NUMERICAL VALUE OF MY THOUGHTS

Sumnima Adhikari

To order additional copies of this book, contact:
Xlibris
1-888-795-4274
www.Xlibris.com
Orders@Xlibris.com

Contents

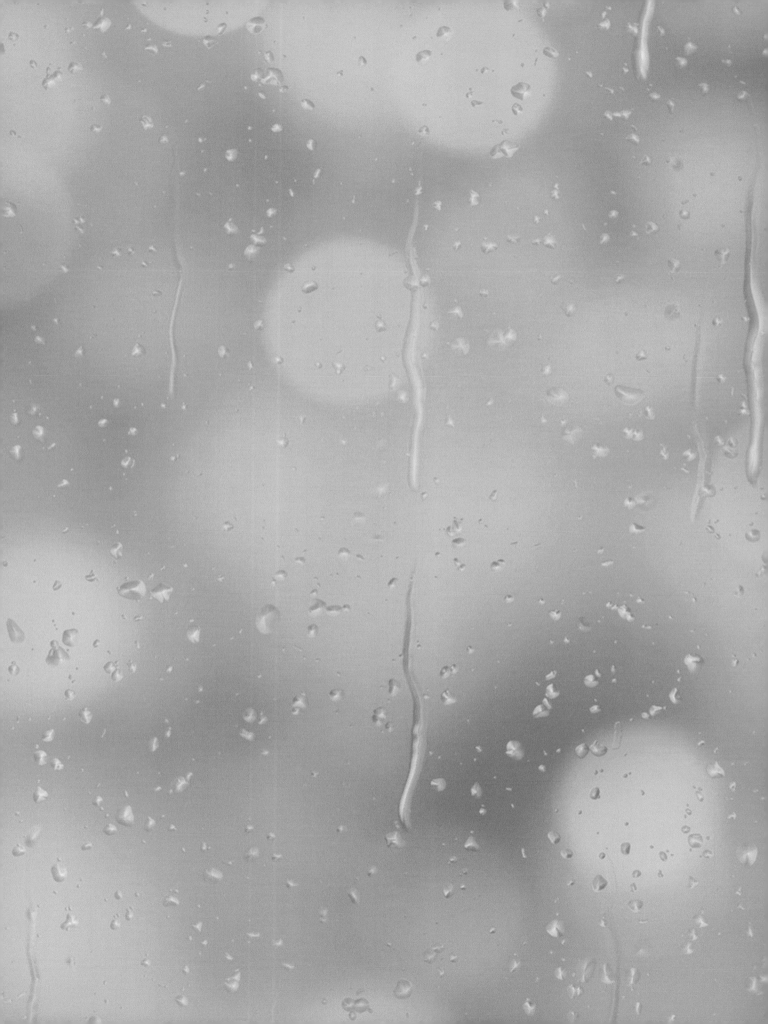

How I Became an Author

Mindfulness has always been a part of my well being throughout my life. Observation and examination of my own thought process has been like a hobby to me. I wonder what I am thinking right now or what I thought just a while ago or what I am going to think after this event has always been a matter of curiosity to me. Am I insane? Yes I am or no I am not. There is always confusion and anxiety regarding this. The level of anxiety is determined by how much we are nervous about ourselves and our circumstances. There's no perfection so there is no cure for anxiety and nervousness. Unless we are sleeping, there's ought to be some kind of feelings inside that keeps tickling us, making us busy. Isn't that what is called anxious behavior?

I had read it somewhere during my childhood that there are only 7 wonders in the world. I was probably around 8 or 9 years old at that time. Since I started thinking why don't I become the "8th Wonder of the World"… literally, yes! Again this was just my imagination! Hilarious but it came from the bottom of my heart so I thought I have to honor it wholeheartedly. I decided why don't I plan on becoming someone extraordinary! Someone with bold point of view about life, a pioneer by free will. No offense to anyone or any circumstances but I had to listen to my gut feelings about what I would become in my life.

I had fascination for so many things during that age that I couldn't decide what I would be. I knew it would be very challenging for me to challenge myself to be someone so authentic (Atleast that's what I always thought about geniuses). I realized that the best way to find ideas would be to read books, read books here and there, everywhere. Whatever I found, I would just start reading. Sometimes I used to read books so much that I used to get severe headache but at the same time lots of ideas used to spur in my head. So much that I would just be overwhelemed with ideas. I wish I had jotted down all those ideas that came into my mind at that time. I regret! But, I always go by the fule "I'ts never too late" to inaugurate anything. That's why I never gave up an idea of becoming an author. Not just an author but I wanted to write something honestly interesting, something "out of the box". I wanted to write about my thoughts so accurately that people could literally visualize what they might be missing out when it comes to enduring their thoughts or point of view about life and the overall Universe.

I knew that authors usually follow some definite rules and are usually quite educated with masters degree, double PHD..wow!.. But, I wanted to be the type of author who can give confidence to anybody or anyone to start writing their heart out. I decided that I will make people understand that there is no barrier to what you can think, what your thoughts prevails you and how our thoughts lead us to the direction we are supposed to be heading. Since the day I realized that I should write everything that comes in my mind, I have started typing and writing as fast as my mind ponders and wonders!1 This has also helped me type fast…haha!

Until now, I was probably banded by some boundaries, shame, culture issues, etc. But, now I feel that the time has come. I can be me and think freely at all times. I have also realized that my thoughts are quite precious. So, that's how this book happened. Since this was going to be my first book, I wanted it to be something different. In some way, I wanted this book to be the reflection of me. I believed that my Imagination, my perspective about life is unique and needs to be shared. Being misunderstood has always been the hardest part of my life. So, I always wanted to write so that I could share my ideas in such a way that people won't freak out when they see me or try to talk to me. I was born this way and it would be great if you could accept me the way I am is the main reason I wanted to jot down my thoughts in this book.

I think that more than anything, people just ignore their thoughts and don't even worry about it. But, throughout my life I have always felt that God lives in our thoughts. God in my dictionary is an imaginary statuette who is always there for me no matter where I am or what happens to me. This is the reason I started concentrating on what comes to my mind. What does actually prevail me to think? Why is my imagination so intense? Why am I so satisfied with what I think and feel? At one point in life, I realized that it wasn't just me buy my English teacher showed me my essay about "Imagination" to everyone in the class and the whole school declaring that it was one of the best essays he has ever read. I was overwhelmed with joy. My confidence tripled at that time. Encouragement of any kind is the best fuel to light up the balloon of success and let it fly with assurance. When it comes to writing, I never feel discouraged or disgraced. I am always in a jolly mood when it comes to writing.

They say pain makes you overthink. I didn't use to believe it but now I optimistically believe that pain triggers the overthinking process. What could be more painful than to be lonely? This has been the most painful reality of my life that I have lived alone and fought every battle alone. Staying away from family and friends could be lethal for a normal human being. It was quite detrimental for my mental well being but as they say, there needs to be a crack for the light to enter. I saw so much light in this darkness that it is unexplainable. I must have been the luckiest person in this world to be so mentally stable even after going through so much of crisis an unusual circumstances. My next book will be about my past life, my divorce drama, my adventures, heartbreak and everything I have been through since my childhood. I wouldn't stop writing.

The overthinking process got so triggered in my brain that I started doing completely different things to forget my pain and loneliness.

I didn't want to kill my unique personality even thought it was getting tough and to keep going with so much burden and heartache so I found that the new way to kill boredom and sadness would be to write the overwhelming thoughts that appeared in my mind every moment. I am so proud of myself that I didn't lose my mind during that process and that I always found hope some somewhere each time.

I give credit to the internet and social media for keeping me busy and involved too. I chose the social media carefully and followed it in every way possible. That's how I got to know people, their different lives, different circumstances and got to compare how my life is different than theirs. I got infatuated by a couple of celebrities, got bullied but overall I was just living my life rather than being bored out of loneliness and sadness. My philosophy is that its better to be crazy than to commit suicide.

Life always has a meaning to it. It is always best to try to discover new ideas from the circumstances you have been given than to end life because of how divergent and weird your life has become. "Accept it" however it is. Dance to it's tunes however the music might be should be the way we should all think about this precious thing called "life". You are allowed to agree to the terms and conditions of life you disagree to those terms and conditions, you can't hit the "next" button and move forward in life. This philosophy has always kept me going and hoping to have this attitude so that it will help me keep moving forward and doing greater things in life.

The following quotes in this book cam straight from the bottom of my heart and has not been copied from any book or writings. Whatever came into my mind, I just started jotting it down. This book is just the collection of those thoughts and imaginations that blossomed in my mind each and every moment. I hope you all will enjoy reading it and please don't hesitate to ask me questions...lots of questions. Thank you very much.

LIFE FACTUALLY:

1. Aren't we all on a vacation mode? Just vacationing in our own spot with lots of adventure. That's all life is about. Take everything as an adventure and turn the vacation mode on!! The name of the vacation package is "LIFE".

2. Take the comfort of your zone to the most uncomfortable places you haven't been yet. This world is your oyster! We all are the same, equally blessed, equally empowered and here to create magic!

3. Get inspired by everything! Coz again, trends will just keep all of us in one box! To be out of the box, we have to think different. Invent a trend sometimes!

4. In the end, its not about how successful we have become but its about how much we enjoyed doing everything that came our way. Did you actually enjoy your food that was on your table this morning?? Do so every time! Smell the fresh laundry even it is the only thing you've accomplished all day!

5. Don't take every opportunity coz everybody wants it but take the responsibility to take the opportunity that many might not be able to endure!

6. New ideas bloom if we actually sort through our mind. In a subtle way, shut down all the theories, all the technologies, look up at the sky, feel the freedom of speech, thought process! Now think with your clear mind and soul. That is going to be the seed venture, absolutely brilliant new idea.

7. Let your imagination lead but don't let it slip away from your hand. Remember that we can't let our mind or the artificial intelligence take over us. That would be the worst situation for the human life if AI actually overtakes our mind and soul.

8. While you are climbing the stairs, don't forget to look behind. If you don't remember how to go back to where you left then that's considered as vague success which means that you have the potential to climb up but no integrity to take the flight back home.

9. Believe that it is not your job to please everyone around you!! You cant and its ok. You have you! Just don't forget yourself! That's all that matters.

10. As you get older, it is obvious to get less attention and have the potential to lose charm externally but what is internal never goes out of style. Build your own style and significance internally. Be bold in your ideas and always stand for what is right "for you".

11. Life gets boring when you have to deal with people who don't belong in your life. Leave them alone just like how you would leave the unnecessary clutters of your life.

GENUINELY FEMINIST BY BIRTH:

1. Girls, don't laugh when your boyfriend or your husband makes fun of the girl next to you. He is sexually harassing her and you shouldn't be part of it..thats how one woman can help another woman.

2. Don't ruin a woman's life because you want that man! Be sincere to another woman. That's how we stop looking stupid and more like the men who have been ruling this world for so long.

3. Women don't need to go against men to be powerful! Men are usually cool with women who don't use their body parts to win over the world. Think like a man! Period!

4. Our daughters are born equally strong! Just the way we manipulate them is different!

5. Why is the punishment for being caring is equal to less pay? What crime have women done that they are paid less in the same profession? There are other ways to make babies. Sexual assault happens because men have more monetary transactions than women. Women have to surrender to men to get all the benefits of being intellectual. Equal pay is the way to go! That way both men and women can buy roses for their partners on any given day!! Men on top or women on top, it's the same thing and actually it feels good when both get a chance to be on top and feel the power!!

6. The worst and the biggest dilemma for every woman is, to be the Princess or not to be!!

7. I think women are meant for multitasking! Lets do it in style. If we wanna see more women in offices, solving problems, we need cocoons and comfy loving environment for those unexpected situations we have to face when our child gets sick. Our maternal instincts should not be sacrificed while solving problems but instead manifested in such a way that women can multitask! They should not be given the mental torture of scarifying one over another. They should not be forced to feel hollow and heartless while taking care of their career.

8. Every woman's problem: you go out and about, be ready to explore. Outcome? Finds the fact that this world needs a lot of renovations to gain that respect and justice to all women equally.

Mission fails. You end up fighting for your rights more than what you have to offer to the world. Your enigma, your expertise is quite important. You know that very well but is unable to execute it in the right way because of the lack of proper stabilization of equality between men and women.

9. A woman spends 75% of her life nurturing others and yet the respect level has just been 25%. If she actually gave a damn about others, the force that she possesses is more than enough to be equally intelligent or even more intelligent than men. But because of those few good men, those great sons and those few wonderful husbands, women have to suppress their full force so that they don't disrespect those good men. How ironic! That is called harmony. Nature provides that harmony so that there is no war.

10. Being in love is not for the one you love. It is a condition, an attitude in itself. Just think, would you rather be "in hate" or "in love". Always a winning situation, as long as you're "in love". People who take love as winning or losing have no idea what love actually is.

11. Think like a barbie sometimes. Don't know where she works but the way she managed to maintain her hair, dress, body and still own a beautiful furnished home is the kind of skill every woman should possess. Think about a way to understand what truly makes you super confident.

12. Having an affair with clothes helps you cover up your dignity. Dress up when you step out.

13. Sometimes beauty is exploited because of its attractive nature but even an attractive person has to work hard, earn a living and live with dignity so its not fair to exploit them for being so sexy and attractive.

14. There is nothing more attractive than an "honest man". No matter how handsome you might be, if you are a liar, it is a total "turn off". Men can learn from this.

15. Thinking like a man doesn't make us macho or less of a woman but in fact, it helps us understand men and bring more equality between two entities. Being bold doesn't mean being a lesbian. It just means that bold women care little bit more than what women are created for. They want to be part of the real world, bring a change and use their brain more than just their feminine characters. Men like the women who are less powerful than themselves but that day will come when men will respect those powerful women in the same way they respect weak or outwardly super feminine women.

16. Today #metgala dresses made me realize how every girl can be a "Queen". We love dressing up girls! Yesss! Men will come and go, love for dresses and beauty lasts forever…keep it up!

17. How do we judge a man who is so much in love with his wife and yet can't stop cheating on her? It is beyond our understanding. Stop giving power to them? I guess that should do it.

18. Read me! Understand me! I want to be your favorite book!

19. Don't know about others but my biggest fear is what if we keep losing smart/honest gentlemen in this world? World will be in crisis.

20. Sorry if I couldn't please you. Gosh! Tired of trying to please everyone. Ever wondered if anyone has made an effort to please me genuinely? That would be so great.

21. Having a desire is the basic human need. Do not tag it negatively…..period!

22. Wear a robe when needed! Its better than to stay naked for too long!

23. What is beyond your control is not your fault. Love the love so much that even if you don't get love in return, you can still be fine. Life is quite interesting. Observe it, smile about it, entertain it, thrive to live for it, don't question too much about it. Loving yourself is love too.

24. Men, women dare you to love and respect powerful women.

25. Women need equal pay so that they don't have to beg for financial security with their boyfriends/husbands. Whatever the performance might be, women need equal or more pay than men. It's about time women take the power to save those innocent girls from being raped for financial security.

26. One man deserves to be king and treat his woman as a queen. One on one and that's all. Rest of the women don't need to be spare unless its their choice. "Women are not spare tires".

IS IT LOVE OR NOT! RELATED? NOT REALLY...

1. Relationships are complicated because of the roles you have to play. A girlfriend has to act little bit weaker than her partner to get that sympathetic attention. In the changing world, that could be difficult for girls to portray. Hence, we have more divorces, break-ups, so on and so forth. Fingers crossed for the 21st century relationship rules.

2. To create relationship with yourself, we all need some self-time. Relationship with others doesn't necessarily guarantee enlightenment or better life. Enjoy the company while they're around and don't forget the relationship you have within yourself.

3. Love has no definition, don't try to describe it with words. 75% feelings is involved in the institution called "Love". Enjoy the feeling. Also sex is just 5% in the definition of love. Evaluate the longevity of a relationship accordingly.

4. Every relationship should come with a strict instruction about which movie are we going to be following or which movie scene etc. That would solve the problem of confusion about what the relationship is about.

5. Love is something that prevails when everything else fades away.

6. When I am with my love, I just forget the rest of the world for that moment. At least that's how it is supposed to be. The moments you spend in loving someone is never a waste of time.

7. How to drill someone who is so close to you without offending them? Determine the perfect time and always follow the gut feeling.

8. Passion is the only thing that will help you rejoice everything you do. Be passionate in everything that you put your hands on. Feel the magic of your touch, execute your power in the best way possible.

9. How to solve the mystery of confusion while in love? Express the feelings openly. Look into their eyes, just do it! Love is the only thing that will help you be honest. It is the present moment that counts.

10. Never miss a chance to give a shot at love! That is also an opportunity to feel great about the whole thing called "Life". Never regret those moments of love either! Learn from it but never dismiss the idea of falling in love again! Let it be numerous! Love is your statement and that's it!

11. You lose it and you find yourself again and again. This is just the process of falling in love. The gravitational force pulls you down faster when you are actually in love. You just hold on to your heart, cross your fingers, hope it doesn't get squeezed too hard. After all, it is not a jiggly puff you know! Hold on to your hearts until you know that special someone wont treat it like a jiggly puff!

12. If you wanna see your woman beautiful, relaxed and happy, learn to pamper her accordingly. Personality alteration is also one of the qualities of beautiful woman.

13. Your loved one only wants your undivided attention. That's the biggest gift you can give the one you love. Away from everyone and everything.

14. A child needs a lot of security. A secure child is able to put the best efforts in everything he/she does.

15. About honesty and trust: A person with single status and multiple partners is more faithful than a cheating person committed to a family. Trust is not blind folded. It requires authentication and integrity.

16. The status of a person depends upon how they like to work things out. But you don't judge that person you have chosen too much. That creates confusing problems in our minds. You wanna be with that person and yet have so many judgement against that person and this is the quickest way to be sad in life.

17. When you are confused about a person's character, be kind to that person for a while without judging. Even then, if you have negative feelings for that person then it's not good but if the negative feelings goes away then its heaven.

18. Sensitive people tend to alter their personality all together to prevent themselves from getting hurt. It's their life long wish to never get hurt, to not be shattered by wrong approach from people they encounter. The whole face, skin color, even the posture gets altered and the only personality they portray is how they should be reacting while people treat them. This is also called intelligence. Most intelligent people also learn to master the skill to disguise themselves according to the situation.

19. The dept of understanding for human culture and relationship is what brings us together. How do we make it more respectful and genuine. How long are we going to be rumbled around the complication of human relationship only.

20. As soon as you make a friend, don't plot ways to underestimate him/her and feel superior! Let others grow in your friendship.

21. A friend in a bad situation is not your "slave". If you can't be their friend, or can't uplift them, don't hurt them but just leave them alone.

22. The only definition of family is, they are the brick and cement to help you build a rock solid safe haven!! If they are just up to bringing it down, you are better off without them!

23. How many people can claim that they can fall in love everyday with different people, for different reason. At least I can claim that I don't hate people. Some people only deserve hate but I still find a reason to love them.

24. Don't enjoy laughing at somebody else's pain and suffering. You might be winning at that for now but may not be able to win forever. What goes around, comes around!

25. Education is great but it makes you so damn brutally honest person that its hard to "fit in" among all the bunch of liars…hahahaha..hehehehe…having fun and lying and ****ing around! Yikes, this is when education hurts. As you become more and more knowledgeable, it becomes hard to fit in and as a result you end up being an outstanding person….like literally out-man-standing-alone! And the worst thing is, the same liars will try to prove you wrong, each time and life becomes a battlefield. If you happen to be fine in this battlefield, you become lucky, otherwise, you can't enjoy. Either way, learning to survive is the best way to deal with any situation.

26. I wanna be a fool, be high, forget that I know so much, ignore all of your mistakes, let it be, just so that I can hang out with you (situation these days!!) If only I could achieve this special tactic of being a liar, I would have friends lined up to hang out with me. Hitler had millions of followers and Jesus/Buddha had 8-10 followers. Its hard to be perfect and have friends who are imperfect. You get feeling that you might be offending them. You're too perfect, go away!

27. Don't make anyone wait too long coz while they are waiting, their brain keeps talking to themselves. They will keep thinking, some will even overthink and during that time you could be one of the negative prospect. I'm sure you wouldn't like that, would you?

28. Friendship is a genuine relationship, don't expect it from fake people. Genuine people are everywhere, observe optimistically and keep up the good work.

STRICTLY LOVE I THINK..!!

1. Bringing people and things together is what love is about. You can't promise love without the existence of viscosity. Viscosity here means bringing two people so close to each other that they forget their own identity and just blend in with each other.

2. If you want a company to accompany you, don't wait for the similarity. Hold that person's mind with an appropriate approach, transfer the ideas from that person's mind, filter it through, delete the ones that are used up or useless! Now, keep only the fresh idea, multiply that fresh idea, find a way to execute it in the best way possible. Always remember, one idea can change your life.

3. When you actually love a person, that person can feel it by the way you hug him/her. Take the movie "Avatar" as an example. You actually exchange feelings while you are hugging and holding somebody's hand. You feel confident by the way you hug each other.

4. Marriage is not a competition between two people. It's got nothing to do with success or failure either but yes, bliss in marriage is what keeps the depression, anxiety, sadness away and hence success comes to those who know how to be happy and smile. A partner is supposed to be there to help you relax, not to drill you- to show you the positive side of life, not to offend you.

5. You might have a big heart (I mean, literally big heart) but it is always a great idea to remember that you cannot be deeply involved in two different love affairs. There's a chance of both getting hurt during this time and it could be a health crisis too.

6. As much as you love someone, be respectful to their feelings too.

7. A man loves to see two women fight with each other for him. This used to be passion in olden days with kings. That's why a king believed in marrying two or more queens. The same formula applies to men in this modern era who believe they are the king. It might be psychologically very tantalizing and arousing game of love for human being.

8. There is a thing called autism due to friends. We could call it "Frautism". This is the phenomenon that occurs due to the bad treatment by friends. They come, give u hopes of togetherness, celebration and happiness. When not around, they don't stay in touch or hit you buzz. And just like that the friendship is over.

CRAP ME IF YOU CAN! YES YOU, TALKING TO YOU LIFE!!

1. Counting the laughter actually balances the pain.
2. Followers will follow you, hypothetically or physically. It is just the matter of visual effects.
3. As you gasp negativity, so you seal positivity into a box. Opening the box needs a key.
4. You gain what you want to gain that you ought to gain for the gain of self.
5. Color is just color, why do we make it a statement or a definition. Let it be!
6. Black is not always dark, it could reflect sunshine and white is not always pure, it could just mean colorless!
7. Without colors life is tasteless.
8. Music gives the awakening to our voiceless mind. Use it to feel awake.
9. Rhythm has no meaning but while in a pattern, it is the heart and soul of music.
10. We can compare peace with noise as long as it is not peaceful.
11. Apple could be orange in certain circumstances but not forever! Apple will always remain Apple!
12. We can manipulate our mind to flex here and there but not our soul. Soul only absorbs the truth.
13. Life is filled with opportunities as long as you have your heart open.
14. Life will sail like the sailing boat towards any direction we like.
15. Thoughts stack up and become accomplishments. It won't create magic with one moment.
16. Smile even when your heart is aching because pain is very infectious and smile flexes the muscles of our face to ease the pain.
17. Let's not give freedom of speech just to the accusers. The truth might be in the speech.
18. Nothing shouts louder than lies. Just because you are quiet doesn't mean you are wrong. Right is always right.
19. All the things that matter is courage. Rest will follow.
20. Never leave a game for others to win. By the end, you could be a game changer.
21. To the point is just a phrase. You need to push the limits to go further.
22. Anything that pretends is not real for if it were real, there wouldn't be an act.
23. You come out polished when you go through the tunnel of darkness.
24. There will always be a way to find happiness as long as the happiness is something that is in your mind.
25. If you are sad, everything else around you will be even sadder.
26. If the better one feels the necessity to challenge the weaker one, who is who might be of great argument.
27. Your strength cannot be measured by numbers, it is a process of living life, not mathematics.
28. You are who you are as long as you don't earn honors. The honorable ones are who they are in the best version of self.
29. Don't mind the surroundings if they don't mind you.
30. Social animals are themselves social, no need to doubt about it. Even in their loneliness they are socially social and in touch with others.
31. Why humans are superior is just a statement. Humans are actually governed by animals.
32. Tough decisions are made by people with Iron heart. The ones who can handle the tug of war are the ones making the decisions.
33. Challenges make circumstances worth challenging. It takes courage to overcome those challenges.

KNOWLEDGE AND MIND IF I MAY "BE"!

1. Grades are not the only thing that counts! When you go to college, you go through that intense process of knowledge gaining attitude, the desire to do better each time, the hopes and dreams! Everything gets accumulated into your brain when you actually make up your mind to gain education.

2. Education is great but it makes you so damn brutally honest person that its hard to "fit in" among all the bunch of liars…hahahaha..hehehehe…having fun and lying and ****ing around! Yikes, this is when education hurts. As you become more and more knowledgeable, it becomes hard to fit in and as a result you end up being an outstanding person….like literally out-man-standing-alone! And the worst thing is, the same liars will try to prove you wrong, each time and life becomes a battlefield. If you happen to be fine in this battlefield, you become lucky, otherwise, you can't enjoy. Either way, learning to survive is the best way to deal with any situation.

3. Born to make an impact says the extraordinary mind. Let it speak!

4. Create a brand for yourself. You are the brand, so unique and extraordinary. And be your own Brand Ambassador. Your world, your life, it's all yours.

VISIONARY BY CHANCE:

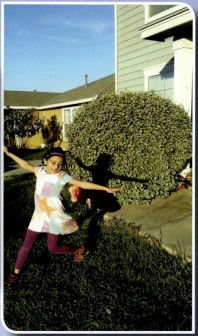

1. Vision is not what you see clearly and completely! Hang on to the half clear, half complete and don't give up until your vision comes alive. Same with your life partner. He will see you even in your darkest hour and will never give up on you until he knows you.
2. 6th sense is real! It is not witchy! It is just extra strength in your brain. All mothers have it and all fathers with motherly instinct have it too! Use it for safety.
3. I wouldn't follow the crowd coz they all are better than me in following the crowd they are in. Let me take it easy, eat, pray, love, and enjoy everything slowly but steadily!
4. The crack in the rock is what will let the light pass through. If you are a crack, you are eligible to shade the darkness and shine the light.
5. The reason intelligent people laugh at more things than others is coz they have figured out that life is nothing more than a joke. You are born and then after all the drama, you gotta die leaving everything behind? You gotta be kidding me! It's a joke so don't take it seriously. Just have fun all the way and stay alert at all times.
6. Kids naturally are born to guide us. My daughter is leading me even though it looks like I am the one showing her the path. She gives me a reason to wake up every morning and accept what this world has to offer with a smile on my face. She is my family, my world!
7. You are the product of all the worst/best/awkward/unusual things that have happened to you. Endorse yourself genuinely.
8. Having the privilege of having lots of kids is not distinction or is achieved with the formulae that we see, it is the combination of luck, wealth and blessings from family. If the foundation is strong, it's worth having more than one kid. Otherwise, everything could just crumble like in a domino effect!
9. I wouldn't do anything with a heavy heart. Which means, you have to be mentally prepared and happy to enjoy doing big task. Stay away from anything that is detrimental. There should be a provision to divorce from your family too. A legal divorce to cut all the ties.

10. Find projects everywhere you go! The best way to get the task done is by finding the right projects and taking care of it in the best way possible!

11. Someone up above is watching over us, he is having fun watching us act stupid. If we don't unite, we will just be fighting at all times.

12. The only mission should be "Peace". Those beautiful women in the beauty pageant really mean it. We all want peace! You create beauty from the beginning by thinking beautiful, by eating beautiful, by being beautiful. Grumpy people are always ugly.

13. Be fashionable so awesomely that whatever you wear becomes fashionable! Its like, who do I think I am?

14. People who are hurt the most, dress up well the most! That's the best way to cover up pain and sufferings! Those people are lucky who feel comfy in whatever they wear. That just means that they haven't been hurt and are jolly in their life. Lucky people!

15. Here comes the challenge! Its more like, oh yeah, you're most welcome challenges!

16. Face the fears without any tears.

17. You are just making history in every step of the way! Each one of us are destined to have our life written in a book for everybody to read for inspiration. Feel special in the life "At present".

18. Humans have addiction to slavery. We like to enslave others but by doing that we are just letting others live our lives. Slaves actually get to represent your life on your behalf. Doesn't sound cool huh?? Play the games of your life on your own, experience it on your own and always remember, sharing and doing things in a group makes the game even better.

19. A talking mind is the product of over-productive, hyperactive, intelligent person without any opportunities. That's why a river looks fresh when it is flowing! Our mind becomes like the stagnant water if held tight without any chance for flourishment!

HOW'S ATTITUDE?...(INSURED THOUGHTS)

1. A person with lots of sad experiences in the past has to depend on those few fun moments/ repeated every other minute in his/her mind to feel better, to feel good. And we call that natural phenomenon "madness" which in our world is given psychiatric treatment so harsh that the pain doesn't get healed and in fact gets worse and worse.

2. Natural cure for any of our feelings that is not suitable or acceptable to the society is to figure out what our body develops in the after math of any kind of such feelings. Some people drink all their lives coz that's all they've figured out. Some people smoke continuously! Some just look for companionship. Others, watch funny movies. But maybe just the way we act could be the cure.

3. Again, controlling something is just like holding back water in a dam. Its not good in a long run. "Letting it flow" is the best way to go.

4. Laughter therapy is nothing to be ashamed of. Laugh at all of your troubles, smile at everything coz that's how our brain creates new ideas. Otherwise, sadness is quite powerful and is able to drown you to the bottom. If smile helps, keep smiling!

5. Downside of finishing first is that you could get bored of all those extra time you have. It could actually be illegal, very abnormal. But, never be worried about "standing out"!! Be worried about not being able to finish it at all.

6. When you are trying to flow like a river, those pebbles on the way are just there for bumps to remind you that there are troubles around. You will still keep flowing, have no fear!!

7. Plan is to make things possible, accessible to all. Remember that pearl is found hidden inside shells, diamond only shines when polished, it takes years to age wine and real wood is always found within a tree. Talents are hidden among those unfortunate ones who have been bombarded by troubles of the world. They should all be discovered.

8. This urge to keep moving, to keep going forward is just a reminder that life is too short to not move. Progress is beneficial and stagnant water can't remain fresh too long!

9. Turns out the value of something is not in the price. In my experience, I have found some of the best products that cost me almost nothing at all! Try and discover new things from every point of view. We all came naked into this world so there's no point in putting price tag on anything. It has to be worth it!

10. Life moves full circle at any given point. What goes around, comes around. In this case, patience is the best tool. If you are patient enough to hold onto the journey you have endured, you are eligible to witness what's in store for you in the horizon.

11. Observe the sun when it rises and when it falls in the prey of darkness. Dawn to dusk is the moment of excitement, be-wilderness, little bit of anxiety but whole lot of energy. But the best part of it all is the story behind the beginning of dawn and ending of it. Accept the facts!!

12. Leave room for some imagination in your extremely real life. That's what sets you apart. Your thoughts don't go by rules! And it is what determines how unique you could be. Use your imagination to lead you to your destination, not to prohibit you from being creative.

13. Turns out we are determined to let the artificial intelligence rule over us. Lets stick to each other as humans. Enslave the artificial intelligence not empower them. We ought to let the low paying jobs be done by robots and not program them to do responsible tasks. Humans need to be on the top level. Let the robots serve coffee for us while we magnify the human intelligence. If we let them do bigger tasks, they will empower us and we will be dummies in their world.

14. Cure is in the prevention. I think there is safety measure for every kind of disaster or bad circumstances. And women need more gadgets and gizmos to take care of all of the work they have to do than men do. That is why human are still behind in development coz we haven't been able to provide enough gadgets and gizmos for women who want to take care of everything with so much energy and determination.

15. Friends who enjoy seeing you suffer are being tortured themselves inside. Let them heal, leave them alone.

16. As we grow older, we become more and more racist. We only want people who are in the same situation as us, around us. Don't hesitate to disappoint.

17. People who have known you the least have the most to say about you. Enjoy their evaluation and judgement about you.

18. People who are guilty of being ugly will never be able to see beauty in anything they see. As they say "Beauty is in the eyes of the Beholder". They are addicted to criticism.

19. A cool mind is never suspicious. Enjoy the present moment like you own it. When love comes your way, grab it with all the intensity you can adhere.

I AM POSITIVE IF I DARE...

1. The idea is to get into the character each time. Take the role, take the center stage, just do it!!

2. When you watch a movie, chose one of the character you would like to be in that movie you are watching, be the character and enjoy playing the character virtually for the rest of the movie.

3. Believe that you are in it for real. That is magical and you are the magician.

4. People's opinion matters but they don't live in your mind and heart so let them have an opinion but never let them change your unique opinion. Have enough courage to lead them towards the right direction instead.

5. All of those quirky and absurd ideas that pop up in your mind?? That's all cool. Those are the things that actually make you or break you. Those are the unique version of you, accept them, enjoy them and make the best out of them.

6. Don't worry about where you've been. You can never go back to that direction. Look forward to where you are headed.

7. The subtleness of the human being is their real personality. Their words, actions and reactions, everything is just the reflection of what they are dealing with or who they hang out with.

8. Without the stamp of confirmation, never open up too much about yourself. Your livelihood is very precious.

9. The biggest achievement in life is to be able to flexible and take care of things in the best possible way.

10. There are only lessons to be learnt, no regrets, no excuses, just lessons.

11. The very thought of categorizing human mind is what sets us apart. We all think differently yet, want to treat each other commonly. That is not exactly how it is supposed to be is not even a statement.

12. Some people function with an overloaded mind. That's how they understand world i.e. they indulge everything but filter their mind each and everything they indulge. Think about how our body system works. The waste matter that comes out of our body has been filtered by our system. It has to reset the body to the original position every time.

13. The only time you feel free is when you know it will work out, wherever you put your hands on. That's the spirit of freedom. Guilty feelings or doubt captures our brain in the worst way possible.

14. 50% of our time is wasted thinking about how I can bring some good changes into this world and 50% of my time is wasted looking for love, that secure love that will never be away. Turns out, you end up finding love everywhere but that one particular person haunts you down the aisle, everywhere.

15. Dreams are quite mixed up when it is raw and numerous. But that's what exactly makes you an over achiever. Let the dreams be tangled with each other, let it bore you, confuse you and underestimate you at times. That's all the seed stage of your dreams. It won't let you be free until you take it to the destination. Let it haunt you, shiver if you have to but never lose it's sight.

16. We carry out feelings in our mind as a result of the consequences we face. One way or the other we are all meant to be somewhere. Need for the right time, right moment is what sets it apart from each other.

17. Moving with the flow is an understatement these days. Think about the situation, time and place to make it work. Without special thoughts, nothing can be special or beautiful.

18. Mind and soul divided is another sure way to torture our mind and soul. Concentrating on one situation at a time is what makes it validated or extraordinary.

19. Life is the byproduct of our thoughts. Live it up to the expectations. You think you can hide your thoughts and feelings but what you portray is what your thoughts have processed, accept the facts.

20. We are all made by the facts and figures. Illusion creation is imaginary so never try creating a negative illusion for somebody. Honesty only cares about facts. This is the moment, face it, rise above it, feel it.

21. "When you say nothing at all" sounds very romantic but only up to some point. There is always a melting point and there is always that time when you want to just "give up". Say something or do something before someone gives up!

22. Those who are on the move and want to keep moving will have to stop at one point, pause and collect some memories, think through the moments that are utterly important because what is precious is always valuable and time cannot change the fact.

23. Right decisions are made when you have rested well, eaten well and played an outdoor game with the existence of mother nature. She knows how to help us make the right decisions.

24. A new venture of any kind requires healthy mind and soul. And of course rebooting is quite important too. A loaded mind without any room for reboot is always bound to make wrong decisions.

25. Alpha, beta and Sulphur are the components of any well-being surrounding. If you want to play the game with all of your heart and soul, make a point to decide how much you can indulge yourself into it. Life is too short to waste time thinking about not playing the game whole heartedly.

26. Never try to compete with a person you think you want to fall in love. You will lose for sure coz heart is always the main reason our blood system works. Blood purification is done by the heart. What our heart says is always the right thing to do.

27. Always have such memories in your life that you can laugh about. Cherishing memories is a great thing but at the same time, we all need those incidents that has some hilarious side to it.

28. I truly believe now that the person who is chosen to bring change is always going to be challenged. He/she is given the real game challenge. Video games are just hallucinations. Fun is in the real game challenge.

29. Best way to deal with any bad situation is to bounce back. Let the pessimists torture you during the dark hours. Always bounce back and shine on. Erase the darkness like it never existed.

30. Hold on to the alterations that bring about change. Think about that "very special" person who always makes you smile. Repeat it at all times. Happy thoughts and that special person in your mind is all you need to stay optimist. Life's hurdles could break you down but those special thoughts, that imagination will always help you push yourself forward...

31. What you seek in life cannot be carried out by anybody else other than yourself. Take the responsibility of taking it to the finish line.

32. Remember how you have become a "Star" in other's eyes. Limelight doesn't come for free to everybody's life. You must have done something truly awesome to have come this far.

33. People who travel in pack are insecure to express their individuality. Their weakness is that they feel hollow without the pack.

34. People who think that youth is all about the crazy things we do then you have never been young in your life. Youth is all about using new ideas to stay "Young forever". Young forever doesn't always imply the outer youth. It just means the youthful glow we have in our heart when it's time to have "FUN".

35. A punching bag gets punched at all times because it is unbreakable! You are unbreakable and that's why people love challenging you. Enjoy the challenges!

36. What you consider fun might sound boring for others! That's why you tend to be unique and extraordinary. If you want to stand out, consider all the challenges of being lonely.

37. In the journey of life, you will find people who have over confidence that they can take care of their mind and control yours at the same time. Let them waste time trying to conquer your mind. Be uncontrollable.

38. Here comes 2018! It's just been 02/2018 and already seems like a thrill ride. What just happened?? Things happen and you know overall its got nothing to do with you.

39. The psychology that we keep talking about is not to be read. It is actually just one reason we all need to be sensitive about each other.

40. Figure out why you are here, rest is just your destiny. Once you've figured, everything either seems funny or very much barricaded. Feeling barricaded is just waste of time but its all worth it to think about life as something fun.

WHAT I WOULD REALLY SEEK FOR!!

1. Explore the world with open heart and mind. This world is yours. Broken relationship: here's another chance for you to be single and feel that thrill of finding someone new, someone interesting. Why make life boring when it could actually be quite interesting! When you seize the moment with the one you enjoy being with, life is yours.

2. Everyday is indeed "a brand new day"!! No ifs and buts! Just sail into it like a sailboat. Feel the wind on your soul and move accordingly. It's you who is holding it accountable. Remember, if the boat drowns, its yours.

3. When you actually feel the presence of that right person in your life, relax and just enjoy the moment. Again, there are not ifs and buts here too. It is good and you deserve it all. He will never let you go. This time we like more than 90% about each other. 10%? Who cares! Liking most of the things about each other is a sign of perfect match. There's never 100%.

4. When dreams come true, feel the present moment.

5. We all are just trying to find a way to connect with that special someone whom we love and finding the best way to spend the rest of our lives with that special someone.

6. Different modes in your brain is just a gift. Use it when you need to. Turn the mode on when and wherever it is suitable. The ability to turn the modes on when needed is a sign of intelligence. It is a sign of adaptability that is unique.

7. Never put your happiness in somebody else's hands. That's a sure way to let others take control over your happiness. Take the grip of yourself. Enjoy time being by yourself. Like minded people like to hang out with each other and spend time with each other. Until you find like minded people, stop chasing the monsters who don't understand your ethics.

8. Natural intelligence is humanity. A human being with all the natural instincts will always treat others with respect. Never plot something disastrous for others and always try to provide happiness.

9. Happiness is not provided by others. There is no guarantee to it. So, always look for joy within yourself, either with imaginations, hallucinations, funny moments or anything that could keep you happy and jolly. Without happiness, life cannot keep rolling.

10. So, the education doesn't always mean grades. It actually makes your whole life better, creative thoughts come into your mind, you feel better thinking that you are gaining some knowledge.

At the same time, education recharges your brain to accomplish something higher. You become capable of facing challenges at any level. People throw stupid challenges and all you do is find a escape where education blooms. Its your secret hide out.

11. "Say what you wanna say" is what should be the motivating factor in your day to day life. First, recharge your brain, stimulate it with all the good stuff and there you go boom, you are eligible to say whatever you want and all the good words will flow through your voice.

12. "Smoothie" is the word that actually soothes your soul.

13. People who are single are just always in a vacation mood. When we think about vacation, we think about relaxing spot. That's what happens when we are relaxing by ourselves. Close your eyes and think about how worried you would be if you were actually in a relationship. So, if that really awesome person comes along then its great otherwise, just keep vacationing...!!

14. When you get the feeling that your life is quite adventurous, filled with unique facts and events, you consider everyone as part of your family, whether you like it or not. You just get noticed by everyone, judged constantly, overall, a very busy life. How you ended up this way? It's a funny story. God has created us all differently and I am his special creation. Even in the crisis, I find happiness, unlike other people, I am surrounded by peace and calmness. Vacation mode on at all times.

15. Brain goes whirlwind!! Roller coaster ride but that's alright. This is just the thought process. Knew it was coming and it could happen.

16. For a moment, think that there is no competition around you. Just do what is best. Would you still succeed and feel good about it? Its great to be competitive but not in all situation. Sometimes, just do it for your own satisfaction and not to please someone or something. A couple need to do the same to each other too. They need to support when they can but don't make them compete for love. That's again a psychological disaster.

17. Its great to have fun and ride along but during that time think about how you can bring about some changes in this world. Of course, the good changes. The world is indeed watching. Maybe we are doing something wrong and maybe they are watching over us because of that reason. We need to fix it before it goes overwhelmingly non-fixable. How can we regulate good deeds and not let the dictators win over us. That's the change we need. They are winning so far. Good deeds are underestimated, shamed, brutalized. Bad ones are the ones having fun, doing well.

18. What would be the first thing we would do if we could actually spread our opinion through our mind (just our mind). In today's world, EQ is more important than IQ. With IQ, grades could be higher but ultimately, we need emotional intelligence to govern our ideas and make it of good use. How do we improve our EQ? That should be the main focus right now. After all, stupid people are full of confidence and hence, intelligent people have to stay fearful and nervous at all times. Maybe this is not how it is supposed to be. Maybe that's why Alien invasion is getting so real. They might want to just fix our problems. Maybe they know we are doing something wrong in this planet.

19. Amazing things happen when you get approval from life.

20. Every weird someone could be a potential genius.

21. Let's compare goodness, not people. Every one of us are unique in our own way.

22. God is everywhere in the nature as long as we can feel the presence. We are governed by this system.

BEING LIMITLESS!

1. How you understand the situation is where you will find the answer. Understanding the truth is the answer.

2. We have two situations. One is when we do things as a choice and the other is when we do things to fulfill it.

3. We rejoice when we succeed but sometimes rejoice in failure too. It might just be another step towards success.

4. We all try to point fingers at others, not realizing the fact that we are the ones at fault sometimes. No individual is perfect and trying to be one is a waste of time.

5. Talent is, the ability to create talent in something everyone else see as a Terrain. A diamond doesn't shine at the first glance…mind it!

6. If you haven't got the best result yet, the hope still prevails! BE CONSISTENT! The best is yet to come my friends.

7. Having deep thoughts about everything is a trait or a disorder? What do we consider this type of mindful situation? Is it really that bad or maybe our brain is actually able to build its own hard drive into the system. In many circumstances, by just a person's presence, I have been able to go back in time. Just the touch of that person has made me go back in time and see the whole picture from that point of time. Is this what's called "Time Machine" maybe?

8. Maybe we all can save everything like files in a hard drive. Delete when needed, reboot, understand, go back in time….etc..etc…

9. When brain is loaded with thoughts and ideas, is it really that bad to execute the real circumstances? Or, maybe we are actually able to act out a movie in real life. Just watch the movie and portray it into the real world.

10. Love teaches us how to be patient in an impatient circumstances. He is taking sometime on thoughts. Giving himself enough time to ponder. I am learning to be patient, calm and relaxed. Love is inevitable.

11. It is absolutely more effective when it comes to executing an idea when you are actually sure about something. Why does it have to be confusing all the time? Are challenges just the wishes that is waiting to be fulfilled? Questions, questions and more questions. Are they all going to be answered? Maybe not but still it doesn't hurt to actually question.

12. Why is there always "gang" involved when it comes to doing something wrong? A lonely person is always confused, worried, underestimated and overwhelmed by thoughts and weird ideas. So, basically we are just slaves of our thoughts. But isn't it better to be slaves of our thoughts than just be involved in a gang of bad people. As they say, "Walk alone if you must or if the crowd is headed toward the wrong direction".

13. How you understand the situation is where you will find the answer. Understanding the truth is the answer.

14. We have two situations. One is when we do things as a choice and the other is when we do things to fulfill it.

15. We rejoice when we succeed but sometimes rejoice in failure too. It might just be another step towards success.

16. We all try to point fingers at others, not realizing the fact that we are the ones at fault sometimes. No individual is perfect and trying to be one is a waste of time.

17. Talent is, the ability to create talent in something everyone else see as a Terrain. A diamond doesn't shine at the first glance...mind it!

18. If you haven't got the best result yet, the hope still prevails! BE CONSISTENT! The best is yet to come my friends.

19. Having deep thoughts about everything is a trait or a disorder? What do we consider this type of mindful situation? Is it really that bad or maybe our brain is actually able to build its own hard drive into the system. In many circumstances, by just a person's presence, I have been able to go back in time. Just the touch of that person has made me go back in time and see the whole picture from that point of time. Is this what's called "Time Machine" maybe?

20. Maybe we all can save everything like files in a hard drive. Delete when needed, reboot, understand, go back in time....etc..etc...

21. When brain is loaded with thoughts and ideas, is it really that bad to execute the real circumstances? Or, maybe we are actually able to act out a movie in real life. Just watch the movie and portray it into the real world.

22. Love teaches us how to be patient in an impatient circumstances. He is taking sometime on thoughts. Giving himself enough time to ponder. I am learning to be patient, calm and relaxed. Love is inevitable.

23. It is absolutely more effective when it comes to executing an idea when you are actually sure about something. Why does it have to be confusing all the time? Are challenges just the wishes that is waiting to be fulfilled? Questions, questions and more questions. Are they all going to be answered? Maybe not but still it doesn't hurt to actually question.

24. Why is there always "gang" involved when it comes to doing something wrong? A lonely person is always confused, worried, underestimated and overwhelmed by thoughts and weird ideas. So, basically we are just slaves of our thoughts. But isn't it better to be slaves of our thoughts than just be involved in a gang of bad people. As they say, "Walk alone if you must or if the crowd is headed toward the wrong direction".

25. Unknowingly or knowingly, understand that people will get used to you. They will get used to hating you or loving you, doesn't matter! Make them be used to you!

26. The only person I wanted to be was "Someone". You know when you are overwhelmed by so many talents and that's all coz I have the tendency to feel never confident, or satisfied or settled.

27. Always find ways to convert sadness into happiness. There's no point in feeling it so deep. Be honest to yourself, rest will follow.

28. When the gold actually glitters, feel the shine! Its ok to shine sometimes.

29. Think that you were actually born to live. Have you actually lived yet? How many times have you realized that you have lived or have actually felt the existence of life? This is it so live the life you got.

30. Don't let the toxic people ruin your tranquility. Your well being is based on how balanced you can be. You cant win over them with your goodness. They're just toxic. Just think about all the goodness you possess.

31. Complete tranquility and peace cannot be achieved but still some of us are bejeweled with that quality to bring peace wherever we go. Thank God, he knows where to send those angels to bring peace and harmony where needed.

32. "Complete satisfaction" is what we all are looking for. And there's no such a thing as that. But trying to attain that is what keeps us going. During the process, don't turn evil. You can be good and can still achieve it.

33. If people take you as competition and enjoy winning over you then always think that you are in a very high position where it is impossible for them to attain. So, the only way they can be satisfied is by winning over you. That's why they are after you!! But you are "not in competition" with them. So, never mind, no worries.

34. You don't have competition! You're just improving everyday, getting better everyday, learning new things everyday. Along the way, they will take you as competition, take pride in that. But you wont take them as competition and that will keep you cool.

35. Is daily routine really effective? Or is it just going to limit us from achieving more than our capabilities? More likely, it is going to limit us! To be unlimited, it is important to be flexible, adaptable and divine.

36. Realization of a boring situation makes you figure out how to reduce boredom or even to get rid of a boring situation. Admit it when you are actually bored. People who get bored tend to find creative and new things to "not get bored".

37. If you suspect you have been poisoned, act like you have been poisoned. The one who has tried to poison you will actually enjoy to see you get weak because of the venom. Stand right back into your feet and that's how you will win! In a way, you just get trained to be more susceptible to anything toxic.

38. The track towards greatness and goodness is very slow and heart rendering! But the "fruit of the labor" is always the sweetest!

39. It is always the best idea to achieve something honestly and with your own hard work and determination. This has a very special significance.

40. Sometimes you have to keep saying sorry to the one who is supposed to be saying sorry just so that they can learn to say sorry. It is like a reflection to them. Hello! R u sorry too?? Or maybe not! Oops!

41. We all have our own purpose in life. It's better to not compare purpose of each other with each other's purpose.

42. Do not feel guilty about your thoughts. They are precious no matter what. Just learn to filter the thoughts and express only the ones that makes sense to the world.

FREEDOM OF THOUGHTS!

1. Realize that life wont stay the same always. Everyday is different and new, embrace it as it comes.

2. Be positive! I know its hard but staying positive is the only choice you got right now. Sorry for the interruptions!

3. Sometimes silence is the biggest weapon. Live it up to it! Do not give anyone the pleasure of not letting you safeguard yourself with your biggest weapon.

4. Don't worry if I am doing my own thing, being quiet or just relaxing! Worry about me if I start talking just to please you!

5. "The Sun" is one of a kind, so unique and outstanding. That's why everyone are focused on it. Only "The Sun" could get so much attention, no one could, be proud of it! Take the challenges if you need to but always remember the extraordinary features of "The Sun".

6. Life does justice to people who can't stop living life to the fullest. So focused that they have "no time for hate".

7. "Recalculating"! This is the main formula to keep reconstructing, re-planning life. Life and death both are uncertain so livelihood shouldn't be taken seriously either. Take it easy when life takes different turns.

8. There's always a very good reason why you don't get what you want. It might disappoint you now but the ultimate result is always for your benefit. Life is never cruel to anyone. It is all based on the choices we make.

9. If something is meant to be, it will happen by hook or by crook. Sometimes just sit down and laugh at what has happened to you. It was all meant to be. This is your life story. Something to be proud of. God willing, he is the one doing the magic. If I want or not, life wont stop being interesting coz life could be boring otherwise. Blame it to the boredom.

10. No matter how much you try, some things can never be optimistic. Accept the facts.

11. How can anyone break something that keeps reformatting and reshaping its entity? That's the solid feature we should possess. Be flexible enough to be unbreakable.

12. Goodness just has double "O"s in it. It is actually GOD ness. So, you don't actually have to be at the church, mosque or temple to find God. Find it right where you are, be good!!

13. Those who are born rich are the luckiest ones. Agreed! But those of you not born so lucky? Think about the experiences. Those rich born kids don't have the privilege to experience and learn how to rise in crisis. That's a sure way to a defeat for them. But the tough ones, the experienced

ones are unbreakable! Learn from the experiences, don't feel the burn. Feel lucky in the way you are. No one needs to suffer.

14. Take the responsibilities seriously. Its better to run with the responsibility than run away from it.

15. Feeling empathetic even about tiny things keeps us busy and hence, boredom goes away. Feeling empathetic is being in the present moment and it is always the best thing to happen.

16. Still in the game! Holding on! Never quitting! About to score…oops! maybe not! But I will for sure! This should be the attitude about life. Remember, attitude is the heart and soul.

17. Sometimes imaginary version of a person is more appealing than the person himself. The dilemma is to either love the imaginary version or the real version! The point is, don't make your friends love the imaginary version of you, be real, be original.

18. How do you make your thoughts "Precious"?? Simplify it, let everyone listen to it.

19. If you don't have anything to do. Sometimes just sit down, relax and just wish! Wish for good life, wish for wealth, wish for happiness, wish for crazy things! Don't worry, just wish! Wishes are like the model structure of our life. Wish about something so hard that it has no other choice than to be true!

20. How do you play the game of life? Try including everyone into it! Best ones, worst ones, bad ones, good ones, ugly ones, beautiful ones, everyone need to be included into it. A game cannot be played alone. Now, enjoy the game of love, the game of life! Interesting it is.

21. Adding values into your life makes a lot of sense but sometimes, it gets very necessary to subtract some of the unnecessary things to declutter life. Declutter friends too if necessary!

22. When you don't have enough resources, use your imagination! That's the best way to keep up the good spirit. People who have nothing have the most creative mind and its all because of their imagination. Let it rise up to the new height!

23. Global citizenship should be a thing. Just like liberal people in politics, a global citizen would have a right to be the citizen of any country or take any culture as theirs. This would be the most helpful way to bring peace into this world.

24. The greatest privilege for an honest person would be to be scanned in and out about their life. It's a disaster for a thief but a blessing for an honest one.

25. You don't always do things to show. Sometimes, you just do things to keep adding blocks to build your life.

26. Each and everyone who come into your life has a different role. Let them play the role they are supposed to play and move on. Don't expect anything. You are the Heroine, the Queen of your life no matter what. They are just supporting actors and actresses who have a very few acts to play. You are leading your own life and should have the potential to lead. If your Hero, your King comes by, that's great and the movie of your life will be even more complete but until then play the role of the leading actress in the best way possible.

27. When people don't care or mind you, mind your own business. We all have a destiny and purpose in life. It's not that God has chosen only one person to be successful and the rest will be dying with poverty. We all are looked after by nature, we all are equally loved.

28. Don't let anyone define the meaning of your life. Absolutely no one can. Your life has to be lived by you, discovered by you, adhered by you, loved by you, accepted by you and explored by yourself!! Be patient and see what you got and where you are headed! Do not copy coz then that wont be the original life of yours.

29. Be limitless in learning something new. Always say huh??! Rather than being too confident and saying oh yes, I know! Don't be confined by the culture you were born with. Yes, that's your identity and dignity but refusing to accept other culture is like barring yourself from gaining more knowledge. Always leave a room for more knowledge.

30. Have so much will power that wherever you might be, you gather the courage to be patient enough to plant the seed and let it grow with time.

31. Respect your enemies and listen to them. They are the ones who can show you the ultimate reflection of your weakness. They are the perfect mirrors of your life who can help you correct the blunders and save you from going to the wrong direction. Be comfortable around them.

32. When you are among the selected few and you feel the burden of taking the responsibility, relax and be authentic in doing it. That's all it counts.

33. Dare to head towards the unique direction where not even a single mind can dare to imagine venturing. Our originality is the sole purpose of a new discovery, new invention. Be bold enough to accept these facts.

34. Remember that life and situation is constantly changing. It wont remain the same is the attitude you need when things go wrong and I will maintain this situation should be the attitude when things are going really well.

35. Before completely giving up, think about why you even started at the first place or why you came back, tried again, or why your heart never gave up??

36. A pearl in the oyster resides alone, so calm, perfect and shining. Its hard but precious things have to always stay alone to stay unaffected, unharmed, protected. When you are alone, imagine that you are the pearl.

37. Always listen to the nature, understand how it works. That's where creativity gets generated from.

38. A performer doesn't have to worry about convincing people. That could constrain his creativity. Sometimes its best to just keep performing without worrying about the impact of judgment.

39. Make your boredom the fuel for new discoveries.

40. Employers should stop getting reference from their employee's friend circle. How do we know they're not plotting against us? That could be detrimental to the career of a hard working, self-sufficient human being.

41. Get to the destination of your success like a "Dark Horse".

42. I always wondered if the Superman actually wore extra underwear under that outer underwear. I hope he did…lol..!

43. Ask questions to people who you think are mysterious and not understandable. Its not fair to judge them without knowing what's in their mind.

44. "Lazy genius" is a phrase that could define a person who finds the easiest/laziest way to get to the destination, to achieve success. Don't work too hard to find happiness is their motto.

45. When you find out you are the "Designated Leader", take the responsibility like a pro.

46. Trust me, I am just working on being a "Pioneer". There's nothing awkward about it.

47. Don't tag a genius as God! The word "God" scares normal people but what they don't know is that genius is achievable! So, being like God is possible for everyone. I truly believe that it is just a thought process, nothing gifted!

48. Please don't lose your sleep to gain something. The tired mind is prone to wrong thoughts.

49. Don't try to copy me, it wont suit you. Accept your uniqueness. This world and life is for everyone.

50. Its not always true that you execute what your thoughts generate. We do need filter to any thought process. Those who don't have filter are in big trouble. Never judge someone by their thought process. Raw thoughts are just like soup or a broth. It's all mixed up! But what you actually portray to your audience is what matters.

51. Always listen to your elders and peers. They have the best ideas that today's generation cannot even think about. Be old fashioned in creating new ideas.

52. In the comfort zone we blossom. Have atleast one cozy pod that makes you feel "oh so awesome". Make it a habit to relax in that pod. Be tough when out and about.

53. Try everything that's in your ability. A player has to learn from practice.

54. You don't have to tag something as "hard work" as long as you enjoy doing it. Hard work always pays off but if you enjoy the journey of the work you do, life pays itself. Every moment is precious and needs to be accepted with full energy and enthusiasm.

55. Its not a bad thing to shake things up! There are only few people in this world who can make an impact! So, accept that special title you have been gifted with and shake things up whenever possible. That's what is called "magic" moment. There wont be that actual wand and twinkling stars falling from the wand. The magic is created by being innovative.

56. The first phase of innovation is that there is the tendency of you being extremely lonely, banned from every parties, looked upon as "weird creature", waved goodbye by every individual, no easy path shown. Second phase might be the same too and the third phase/ the fourth phase etc…etc..but what really matters is that you don't give up even in those difficult phases, situations. That's how innovation becomes a "Creation".

57. Everything needs change with time. There is expiration date to everything and every situation. Men are used to ruling but if the alteration wont be equal or more towards women, there wont be any progress. The way human beings are progressing, both men and women are supposed to be equally participating to maintain the balance. Otherwise, it could be overwhelming to just one entity.

58. Anything you own is supposed to be valuable. Be so authentic in doing what you do that the value of your being becomes more expensive than what you are worth..

59. Life underestimates those people who don't want to rise up. Those are the people who always look fine, never anxious. Its good to be little bit upbeat and anxious about the future to let the engine running.

60. I would rather have a healthy relationship with my imaginary friend than be content with an affair that has no meaning to it.

61. Taking your own path with confidence means discovering yourself, just being the best version of yourself! Along the way, the reflection of yourself sometimes could be taunting and not so "oh so good" and not everyone will understand your path but you would care as long as you know you are headed towards the right direction.

62. "Better you" doesn't always have to be "Approved by all". People understand things at different age. When I was 9, I couldn't any lyrics of any songs in depth. Nowadays, I somehow do understand most of the lyrics of the songs I listen to. Its always a good idea to give time to people to understand our ideas. Let them crawl while trying to figure out who you are.

63. A master needs a servant to be a master. Who is needy here? Need doesn't always mean weakness.

64. The winner is someone who wins his own heart. Proves the facts about himself. Be so original in your identity that nothing else could be more authentic than the whole version of "YOU".

65. A real winner doesn't have to win each and every game. However a winner has to be the "Best" at everything he is and is about to be.

66. "What's going on" is the ultimate feeling you have when you look around and see things around you these days. Whoever feels this way are headed towards the right direction. Those who don't are completely lost creatures.

67. Advertisement usually doesn't cost money…wink wink…!.."Just saying"! There's a trick to it.

68. An Army, a soldier is an attitude, authentic/loyal/superior/honest and most of all an Army attitude never lets you give up. You can fail/fall/fumble/faint but you can never give up! Let's learn these traits from our heroes.

69. How would you pick up those crumbs if it were to break? Things happen, you break, I break but life wont break as long as you have the courage to stand on your feet even after you fall. Welcome to this auspicious occasion called "LIFE".

70. Smile at everything you do. Even when you are in the "Loo", smile that you are actually doing it! Before you sleep, smile that you are about to sleep! Enjoy when you are moving. Play happy songs when you are driving. In the end, the only thing that matters is how much you enjoyed doing things that came along the way. Enjoy those painful moments too. Be content that it helped you learn the meaning of pain and sufferings.

71. Don't be scared to shuffle your situation around. Some people start at the age of 10 and you start at the age of 12. What matters is how well you actually did it when you finally started.

72. Think about it as "Some people die young and some die old" or some maybe live forever (wink, wink). Do we actually have control over everything? The answer will always be "NO". So, live the original life of yours, make some changes here and there but whatever comes your way is mostly inevitable.

73. At what age are we supposed to find "Wisdom" is absolutely unknown. Based on our wisdom tooth? Or maybe it is based on our body structure. So, at whatever age you find wisdom, accept it and mobilize it. Atleast that's what I would do.

74. Love art in such a way that you possess the potential to turn everything into A R T! Articulated Reasonable Tactics! Or in other sense you put your heart and mind into it like you don't believe in anything but the fact that you are going to make it the best. Here's another one: Applauded Rated Treasures! Which means whatever you execute from your heart becomes such a valuable treasure that you get applauded and rated in the best way possible.

THIS WILL BE AT THE END OF THE FINAL PAGE.

• NOW GO HAVE FUN AND ENJOY THE VACATION PACKAGE CALLED "LIFE"

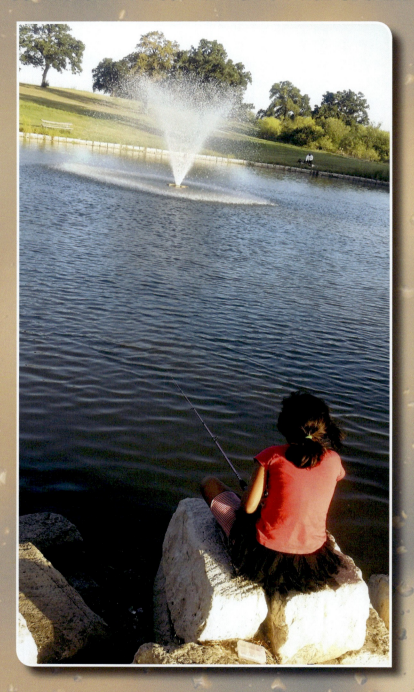

Printed in the United States
By Bookmasters